Victory over Death

Foretastes of Eternity in Prayer

Ronda Chervin

En Route Books and Media, LLC
Saint Louis, MO

5705 Rhodes Ave.,
St. Louis, MO
63109

Contact us at **contactus@enroutebooksandmedia.com**

Copyright 2025 Ronda Chervin

ISBN-13: 979-8-88870-358-8
Library of Congress Control Number:
Available online at https://catalog.loc.gov

Originally published in 1985
by St. Bede's Publications, Petersham, MA

Nihil Obstat:
Lawrence A. Deery, JCL
Vicar for Canonical Affairs, Judicial Vicar, Diocese of Worchester

Imprimatur:
+Timothy J. Harrington
Bishop of Worcester
July 17, 1985

The *Nihil Obstat* and *Imprimatur* are official declarations that a book is considered to be free of doctrinal and moral error. It is not implied that those who have granted the *Nihil Obstat* and *Imprimatur* necessarily agree with the contents, opinions or statements expressed.

All rights reserved. No part of this book may be reproduced, stored in a retrieval system, or transmitted in any form, or by any means, electronic, mechanical, photocopying, or otherwise, without the prior written permission of the author.

Table of Contents

Introduction: "Death Is Swallowed Up In Victory" (1 Cor. 15:54) 1

Chapter 1: "Vanity, All is Vanity" (Eccl. 1:2) 7

Chapter 2: "Fear Not, You Are of More Value Than Many Sparrows" (Mt. 10:31) 15

Chapter 3: "You Are Beautiful, My Beloved, You Are Beautiful" (Cant. 4:1) 29

Chapter 4: "Blessed Be The Pure of Heart, For They Shall See God" (Mt. 5:8) 37

Chapter 5: "That Your Joy May Be Full" (Jn.16:24) 51

Chapter 6: "Perfect Love Casts Out Fear" (1 Jn. 4:18) 61

Introduction

"Death Is Swallowed Up In Victory" (1 Cor. 15:54)

One of my best friends is a contemplative man in his eighties who longs for death. Every day he hopes will be his last. Every night he prays that he will wake up in eternity.[1]

It is not that he is ill or suffering from terrible emotional problems. No. He yearns for death because

---

[1] In *The Church in the Modern World*, a document of Vatican II also known as *Gaudium et spes*, we read these words: "It is in the face of death that the riddle a human existence grows most acute. Not only is man tormented by pain and by the advancing deterioration of his body, but even more so by a dread of perpetual extinction. He rightly follows the intuition of his heart when he abhors and repudiates the utter ruin and total disappearance of his own person. He rebels against death because he bears in himself an eternal seed which cannot be reduced to sheer matter" (§18).

his vision of heaven has become so bright that nothing the world has to offer can compare.

By contrast, I know many religious people past middle age who rarely speak of eternity. Along with unbelievers, they meet each birthday sadly, often refusing to say how old they are. It would seem that their prime of life being over, they think they have nothing to look forward to.

I, myself, am a convert from atheism to the Catholic faith. From my original idea that I was born by chance to a meaningless life, the end of which was to be eaten by worms, I came to the conclusion in faith that I was created in love by Love, to grow in love, eventually to enter a kingdom of endless happiness and glory.

So delighted was I by this surprise that I took it into my head to announce my birthdays in an unusual manner. I'm thirty-five, halfway to eternity! I'm forty-five, two thirds the way to eternity! I hope some day to proclaim one year more to eternity!

So enchanted by the thought of heaven, it puzzles me to find silence about the afterlife so common among Christians. Victory over death is so central to our belief:

If there is no resurrection of the dead our preaching is void of content and our faith is empty too. If our hopes are limited in this life only, we are the most pitiable of men (1 Cor. 15:13-19).

I discussed this with my husband, and he remarked perceptively: "The fear of death is so primitive and universal an emotion that it goes deeper than proofs or doctrines of immortality." He added what I thought at first to be derisive but then realized was serious: "If you could give people a formula to overcome that awful fear … that would be worthwhile."

Stumped for a moment, I soon started to laugh. "There is such a formula, but you won't say it—the famous *pray for us sinners, now and at the hour of our death.*" My eleven-year old son interjected. "You know, daddy, it's true. Even though I don't like the words, when I lie in bed at night scared, I pray them, and peace comes."

Out of this conversation the book you are reading was born. If fear of death is at the bottom of uncertainty of our immortal destiny, then joyful hope must come not from philosophical arguments alone but from a growing trust in God. And might there not be special ways to pray, opening us to confidence in victory, through God, even over death?

Yes, I thought, why not write a book giving ways of prayer that are part of the spiritual life of those who look forward avidly to eternal happiness?

†††

I have gathered such exercises in meditation and contemplation around some favorite passages from scripture.[2]

In the first chapter "Vanity, all is vanity," we will meditate on our experiences of disillusionment in the search for happiness, learning how to cry out to God from the pit of our emptiness.

---

[2] The terms meditation and contemplation are often used synonymously. Technically, meditation is a type of prayer which involves effort on the part of the person praying—one thinks of moments in the life of Christ or composes words of devotion. Contemplation is a pure gift of God. One remains silent with open heart, and God brings grace. In this book, I will use the word meditation for any exercise primarily requiring effort even if it leads into quiet and contemplation, for any suggested prayer primarily made in silence even if it starts out with an image.

In the second chapter, "Are you not worth more than many sparrows," we will consider the reality of spirit in its transcendence over matter. It will include some philosophical avenues to the truth of immortality.

In the third chapter, "You are beautiful, my beloved," we will see how God leads us from delight in his creation to contemplation of his invisible beauty —a foretaste of eternity.

In the fourth chapter, "Blessed be the pure of heart for they shall see God," we will learn how to reorder and purify our lives in conformity with the way of the Lord so that we may not fear the Judgment. Prayers will be given, helpful for self-examination.

In the fifth chapter, "That your joy may be full," we will look at ways of meditating on the joys of earth which elevate the heart to a sense of what is awaiting us in heaven. We will especially consider the hope revealed in the doctrine of the resurrection of the body.

In the sixth chapter, "Perfect love casts out fear," we will find ways to immerse ourselves in God's great love, a love which has gone to the greatest lengths to open the doors to the heavenly kingdom. This final chapter will include prayers to console and elevate as the moment draws closer to victory over death.

Chapter 1

"Vanity, All is Vanity" (Eccl. 1:2)

This famous exclamation of King Solomon, who had everything under the sun that he wanted, finds its converse in the even more familiar phrase "too good to be true."

I wonder at what point a young child first begins to understand the grim significance of those words "too good to be true."

Perhaps a glimmer of its meaning comes on a birthday celebrated in the child's honor when excitement builds to a climax only to end in weariness and tears as the shiniest toy comes apart in the hands of greedy little relatives and friends.

Or perhaps a sense of the sadness of truth comes as the child tries to fathom how loving parents can insist that night after night they make him or her face the terrifying darkness alone.

Why? Why? Why should the long awaited trip to the amusement park be cancelled because delightful rain, which he or she would love to go out and play in, happens to be falling? Why are those bright, fascinating boys and girls at school so mean? Why do his or her parents, each of whom he or she thinks is so lovable, get so grouchy when they are together?

"Vanity, all is vanity." Why does everything betray? The work into which *I* plunged all my youthful energy—how did it get so entangled in fussy details and petty problems that it lost its thrill and became just a job to endure? How did my first love lose its glow? My children change from innocent flowers, young saplings, to resentful teenagers? How did my once strong body become this distasteful, painful burden? How is it that I who gave myself so totally to loved ones now find myself alone? How did my dreams of holiness or heroism become reduced to tired, joyless resignation, holding onto God yet without real hope? For might not the idea of heaven be the ultimate false promise, too good to be true?

Solomon, you who sang the lilting Canticle of Canticles, only to conclude that all was vanity, did you ever wake in the night to hear your father's voice, full-throatedly intoning: "Out of the depths I cry unto thee, O Lord.... hear my prayer"? (Ps. 130:1).

For when many disappointments, congealed tears, have left us numb, if we lift our hearts to God,

Chapter 1: "Vanity, All is Vanity"

suddenly or sometimes slowly, something new begins to enter. A sense or a thought or a feeling intimates that there is divine meaning in the emptiness of our disillusionment.

A great poet, Francis Thompson, immortalized such an insight in the poem "The Hound of Heaven." Christ, the hound, pursues the soul down labyrinthine ways ... with steady beat. "All things betray thee, who betrayest Me," he calls. Yet our sorrows are "the shadows of his hand."

Here are some prayer-poems I, myself, wrote to express an awakening in grace, from despair of myself and the world, to new hope in God:

"My Soul Thirsts for Thee, O Lord"

What is yearning made of?
a rubber-band stretched
from time to eternity?

Not so compact as a wish,
nor as straight as an arrow,
yearning spreads yet
encompasses no object,
bursts through flesh

yet is that flesh's cry.
Yearning, what are you made of?
are you echo of God's sigh?

"Half-Way to Eternity"

O Lord, I love you
with a middle-aged woman's heart
sick to death of flattering
fluttering loves of my own making,
cherishing innocence
as a nearly extinct species!

Your love, too full to be fantasy,
swoops down,
heavy with mercy.

Pinned like a dead butterfly
to the felt cardboard
of my despair
I try to dance to Your song.

A jerky pas-de-deux at best,
garbed in veils of tears.
At last, Your yes wins over my no's.

Chapter 1: "Vanity, All is Vanity"

And so I blush.
Yes, Lord! ever young.
Fill in all the spaces
on the program of my life
and waltz me toward eternity!

"Reliquary"

Human love, so poignant,
must you pall?
your primal freshness
wilt with time?
Must this be ... always?

Yes, my dear, but do not weep.
The tattered garment
stained with blood
can be a relic
treasured as My gift.

Choose me as pall-bearer
of your loves
And I will take them
in my Sacred Heart
to their true home—Eternity!

For Prayer and Meditation

I suggest you select one or more of these exercises as a way to make the themes of this first chapter a part of your own journey to God. If you choose to keep your answers in a separate notebook, perhaps illustrated, this could become a spiritual legacy for your loved ones to treasure after your victory over death.

1. Make a list of the major disappointments in your life. Let yourself re-experience a little of the sorrow of each one, but in every case end your re-collection by imagining Jesus Christ right next to you telling you of some similar grief in his own heart and "wiping away your tears" (Rev. 7:17).

2. Using the phrase "out of the depths I cry unto Thee, O Lord" as a theme, write your own psalm to pray whenever you feel overwhelmed with sadness or depression.

3. Read the poems given in the chapter and fill in your own experiences, praying for all the people who have disappointed you. Include

your own prayer-poem, story, song, or drawing to represent a transition from despair to hope in God.

Chapter 2

"Fear Not, You Are of More Value Than Many Sparrows" (Mt. 10:31)

JESUS CHRIST evidently knew that many of his people simply could not believe that they were worthy of God's notice. With an unmistakable and tender image, he tried to show them that God was interested in their earthly and eternal welfare since he was even aware of the fall of a sparrow or the number of hairs on our heads. As far as I know, there has never been a human lover so infatuated as to count all the hairs on the head of the beloved!

Wrongly thinking of ourselves sometimes as of no more worth than a grain of sand, it is no wonder that we cannot conceive of victory over death, instead thinking that the corpse may be all that will be left: "dust to dust."

Surrounded by a materialistic culture, even the Christian comes to half-think that what cannot be seen is not real. How can we be absolutely sure that we have souls, that the spirit is strong enough to conquer death?

The answer to such doubts is finally given by God to us not with logical arguments but with facts: the raising of Lazarus, the Resurrection of Christ. Before meditating on Scripture, however, it might be strengthening to review briefly the traditional ways philosophers and theologians have tried to show that man's soul is worth so much more than a sparrow, that, once brought into existence, it cannot die.

Consider your essential self, the "me" which persisted from conception to the present. What is this self? It cannot just be the body, for biologists tell us that over a seven-year period every cell in our bodies has been replaced. Yet you are the same person. If not, how to explain memory, culpability, praise? You do not say that the "you" of 1984 remembers a different "you" of 1974. You do not refuse to pay a traffic fine on the grounds that you are no longer the same person or refuse an award because you have changed completely!

But all such continuity of the self means that an immaterial (non-physical) self persists amidst change. This essential self could, then, in principle, continue to exist, even after the physical change we call death.

A further proof that we have a part of us that is not physical is that we cannot measure the soul. A saint does not have a five-pound soul and a sinner a one-pound soul. A thought in your mind is immaterial—a serious one weighs no more than a trivial one, a truth no more than a lie.

What cannot be measured because it has no parts cannot fall apart as does the measurable body of many parts. In death, the measurable, physical part of us comes to pieces. And the soul? By nature, what is not matter cannot be destroyed by matter.

That spirit is different from body, therefore capable of surviving death, can also be shown by examining the soul's tenacity in the face of physical suffering. The following is excerpted from the book *Sermons in Solitary Confinement* by Richard Wurmbrand,[3] a Lutheran pastor tortured for witnessing to his faith and put into solitary confinement for three years when it was realized what "harm" he was doing to the other prisoners in converting them.

---

[3] Published by Diane Books, P.O. Box 2947, Torrance, CA 90509, 1979.

The body needs few things in order to be fully satisfied, simple food, warmth, exercise, rest, and a partner of the opposite sex. My body had all these things (before conversion), but, notwithstanding, I was not happy; I sighed for something more. Who was this "I," dissatisfied when the body had plenty of all that it needed! It was you, my soul.

It was you who wished to know, out of purely scientific interest, about galaxies far away and about facts of prehistory which have absolutely no influence on my bodily state. It was you who delight in art and philosophy, but also in exaggerations and refinements of bodily needs, even when these do harm to the body.

Don't you see, my soul, how right Jesus was in saying that "man does not live by bread alone"? (Now, in prison) I get one slice of bread every Tuesday. And what bread! But I do not just vegetate. I live. I sometimes laugh heartily at jokes which I tell myself, being alone in my cell. I think about politics, about how nations which I have never seen should be ruled. I remember works of art. I lead a life of worship. All this is you. Say, my soul, "I am." You saw me dancing when I was in unspeakable pain. You saw me dancing with heavy chains around my ankles. Who was that one who exuberantly rejoiced? It was not my body. My body had no reason to dance. There was no music to incite it to do so. It was you, my soul.

Take knowledge of yourself, my soul, and take knowledge of your incomparable value. The body will die. Around me prisoners are dying because of the great hunger, the cold, and the tortures, but who has ever seen a soul die? I have lost everything I had in the world, but if you are saved, I shall have kept the pearl of greatest price.

Wurmbrand's stunning argument links logic and experience. Others base their belief on interior experience alone or on exterior facts.

Once, I visited a dying friend in the hospital. I was full of misgivings. I did not want to see this once lively man hooked up to horrid machines, perhaps unable to converse. But when I looked into his eyes, his soul was shining so brightly through them that I was reassured. The intuition of the independence of his spirit from what was happening to his body was so strong that I left him much fortified in my belief in immortality.

Reports of patients pronounced clinically dead but later resuscitated tell of a journey toward a divine light or toward hellish darkness. Patients say they were given a choice to return to the world for a last chance. Scientific documentation, given in the book *Life After Life* by Moody,[4] a medical doctor, who is also a philosopher, indicates that such resuscitated people knew details about what was going on at other floors of the hospital such as information on the charts of other patients which they could not possibly have found out during their time on the operating table. Presumably some kind of spirit-body roams about as part of its journey to the other world.

What strikes me as a Catholic is the congruence between Moody's research and basic Christian doctrine as well as the visions described by holy mystics of their experiences of what takes place in eternity.

---

[4] Raymond A. Moody, Jr., *Life After Life*. NY: Bantam, Bantam, 1976.

It is well known that some contemplatives go into a trance and that their souls seem to leave their bodies. St. Paul wrote, probably about himself, "I knew a man in Christ who, fourteen years ago, whether he was in or outside his body I cannot say, only God can say—a man who was snatched up to the third heaven..." (2 Cor. 12:2-4). There is evidence of bilocation of some saints, where a living person is seen in two places simultaneously.

Most people that I encounter, however, base their belief in the afterlife on experiences of the spiritual presence of their beloved dead. At first, right after a death, it seems that many in their desolation fall into doubt, but then after awhile they find themselves aware of the deceased person being with them. They often talk to them and sense real answers coming back.

As you ponder what has been given so far in this chapter, your response might vary from scepticism to conviction. What I have noticed in myself is that my certainty about victory over death, and with it the separate reality of the soul, depends largely on my own soul's "location" in relation to eternal things. During a long drawn out dying process of a dear friend, I found myself most eager to believe that comfort and joy awaited him. At times when I was in a sort of neutral mood, my thoughts about death would become hesitant, dull. I would shrug my shoulders and think "who knows?" At times when anguish overwhelmed me at the thought of living without him, I would doubt that any good outcome was possible. On the other hand, when, during this same period, I was listening to beautiful music, or gazing at a charming flower, or deep in prayer of quiet, then my own contact with what is of eternal worth would draw me into the milieu where my friend's soul was also sustained. Being in touch with the eternal, the eternity of his innermost selfhood seemed obvious.

Yes, we are worth more than many sparrows. Here are some of the most comforting passages from Scripture assuring us that our eternal life is the will of our Father in heaven:

> The Lord is my shepherd, I shall not want;
> He makes me lie down in green pastures.
> He leads me by still waters,
> He restores my soul…
> Even though I walk through the Valley of the
>   Shadow of Death,

I fear no evil
For Thou art with me… (Ps. 23)

And no man has ascended to heaven, but he that came down from heaven, the Son of man who is in heaven … that whoever believes in him should not perish but have eternal life (Jn. 3:13, 15).

Martha said to Jesus, "Lord, if you had been here my brother would not have died. And even now I know that whatever you ask from God, God will give you." Jesus said to her, "Your brother will rise again." Martha said to him, "I know he will rise again in the resurrection at the last day." Jesus said to her, "I am the resurrection and the life, he who believes in Me, though he die, yet shall he live…Lazarus, come out." The dead man came out… (Jn. 11:32-43)

That they all may be one; as thou, Father, art in me, and I in thee, that they also may be one in us; that the world may believe that thou hast sent me…Father, I will that they also whom thou hast given me be with me where I am; that they may behold my glory which thou hast given me; for thou loved me before the foundation of the world. (Jn. 17:21, 24)

Now if Christ is preached as raised from the dead, how can some of you say that there is no resurrection of the dead? But if there is no resurrection of the dead, then Christ has not been raised; if Christ has not been raised, then our preaching is in vain .... If in this life we who are in Christ have only one hope, we are of all men most to be pitied. But in fact Christ has been raised from the dead, the first fruits of those who have fallen asleep. For as by a man came death, by a man has come also the resurrection of the dead.... For he must reign, till he has put all enemies under his feet. The last enemy that shall be destroyed is death. (1 Cor. 15:12-25)

What is sown is perishable, what is raised is imperishable. It is sown a physical body, it is raised a spiritual body .... Lo! I tell you a mystery. We shall not all sleep, but we shall all be changed, in a moment, in the twinkling of an eye, at the last trumpet .... When the perishable puts on immortality. Then shall come to pass the saying that is written: "Death is swallowed up in victory." (1 Cor. 15:42-54)

For I reckon that the sufferings of this present time are not worthy to be compared with the glory which shall be revealed in us… Nothing can come between us and the love of Christ, even if we are troubled or worried, or being persecuted, or lacking food or clothes, or being threatened or even attacked. These are the trials through which we triumph, by the power of him who loved us… For I am certain of this: neither death nor life, no angel, no prince, nothing that exists, nothing still to come, not any power, or height or depth, nor any created thing, can ever come between us and the love of God made visible in Christ Jesus our Lord (Rm. 8:18, 35-39).

Behold the dwelling of God is with men. He will dwell with them, and they shall be his people and God himself will be with them, He will wipe away every tear from their eyes, and death shall be no more, neither shall there be mourning nor crying nor pain any more, for the former things have passed away. (Rev. 21:3-4)

For Prayer and Meditation

1. Close Your eyes. Picture Yourself falling into a void of nothingness, your body disintegrating and disappearing. Now picture Christ holding your soul in his hands, recognizing it, calling you by name.

2. Have you had moments when you felt your spirit transcend your body? Recall or describe such moments. Then let yourself become quiet and dwell in the sense of your own soul's great reality.

3. Have you ever experienced the spiritual presence of a deceased person? Ask God in prayer to renew that contact, if it be for your good, or to allow you whatever glimpse of eternity might be best to inspire you.

4. Read the passages from Scripture given above, slowly allowing the Holy Spirit to speak to you directly—for example: "Ronda, the Lord is your shepherd. Ronda shall not want."

Chapter 3

"You Are Beautiful, My Beloved, You Are Beautiful" (Cant. 4:1)

THIS LINE IS FROM THE Canticle of Canticles, considered the most exquisite love song of all time. The Song of Songs has also always been considered in Jewish and Christian tradition as an allegory of man's love for God and God's for man.

"Beauty is truth, truth beauty" wrote the poet Keats. For me, it is in beauty that I am most commonly lifted by God out of dull routine into a glimpse of eternity. As the Indian poet Rabindranath Tagore saw it, "The Perfect decks itself out in beauty for the sake of the imperfect."

One day, I was sitting at the beach gazing at the ocean. I heard these words in my heart: "That is Me as ocean." Then the Pacific Ocean shimmered still more beautifully, for I saw it as a part of my beloved Christ. "You are beautiful, my beloved, You are beautiful."

The lyrical insight I had been gifted with that day formed itself into a sort of childlike song: See the bird? That is Me as bird. See the baby's face, That is Me as a child. Then a further surprise: see Ronda? That is Me as Ronda.

I am not a pantheist, God is infinitely more than his creation. Yet he is present everywhere for us to discover. A friend of mine once taught me to ask each beautiful thing I saw what it had to tell me of its Creator. A flower speaks of the delicacy of God in his dealings with us. A mountain reminds us of God's strength, of his eternity. A waterfall might represent the powerful dynamism of God's purity and grace; an animal, God's humor and tenderness. A beautiful face, eyes luminous with love, gives a foretaste of what it will be like to see the saints in heaven. As St. Thomas Aquinas wrote, "beauty is the splendor of being."

It increases my enjoyment of walking down my suburban streets if I praise God for each particular lovely thing I see: the flowers in a garden, the clouds in the sky, the silky fur of a passing cat. I like to believe that God was hoping I would notice these gifts he had left there for me to brighten my day. How disappointing, on the other hand, to plan surprises and have no one open the gifts! "All creation is only one thing, a father clothing and feeding, delighting his child, and saying again and again in everything: I am your Father, I love you," wrote Caryll Houselander, who was also an artist.[5]

Praise is such a prelude to eternity, for in heaven, Scripture tells us, we will join the angels in a symphony of alleluias.

"You are beautiful, my beloved, you are beautiful." Great religious art attempts to portray the beauty of God revealed in Christ, in Mary and the Saints. In painting and sculpture and music, the moral and spiritual values given in the Bible and in tradition come alive for us in the splendor of their beauty.

Many a time, truths of the faith formerly opaque have opened their glory to me through the medium of the arts. It was at the sight of a da Vinci nativity scene that I first grasped the inner essence of the virtue of purity. It was a Raphael depiction of the Resurrected Christ at the miraculous catch of fish that first brought me to belief in his divinity. Listening to the trumpet blasts of the "cum Sancto Spiritu" in the Gloria of the *Bach B Minor Mass*, I felt the Holy Spirit

---

[5] *The Dry Wood*. NY: Sheed and Ward, 1947, p. 172.

enter into me with his gifts, showing me the glowing beauty previously hidden in my prayer forms.

Christian mystics who have had visions, exterior or interior, of the Lord, always describe the intense overwhelming living radiance of his person. The same is true of apparitions of Mary, the Mother of God. So great is the loveliness seen in such visions that the recipient will be willing to undergo any sacrifice for the sake of being able one day to enjoy the beatific vision.

In Isaiah. (65:17), we are promised "a new heaven and a new earth." St. Paul spoke of all creation groaning for the redemption (Rm. 8:22). It is true that we are not given on this earth a clear picture of what the heavenly kingdom will be like: "Eye has not seen, ear has not heard, nor has it so much as dawned on man, what God has prepared for those who love him" (1 Cor. 2:9). Yet many theologians consider that the new earth in the kingdom will include all that is good and beautiful in our present experience including trees, oceans, animals.

One of the most striking literary images I have read about the process of redemption of the material world was in a novel by Charles Williams. The end of the world is imminent. The hero of the novel is walking down a garden path when he sees the shape of a huge bird in the sky. Suddenly, to his amazement, he sees all the birds in the village soaring upward and fusing with the Great Bird on their way to eternity.

Recently, I went on a trip to see a stupendous waterfall near Portland, Oregon. Some of our group were content to view the cascading water from the distance, others increased their delight by walking right through it. It was then that it occurred to me that in heaven, where "all will be one," our experience of beauty will become not only the contemplative joy of seeing created being from afar, but also the ontological ecstasy of becoming one with it. In eternity, I shall know the waterfall from within, for in God I can be part of all things. There will be no separation.

I want to conclude this chapter with excerpts from a poem written by a Sister of St. Francis, Dolores Walker, showing how love of beauty brings us into the foyer of heaven, and based on the *Song of Songs*:

"The Canticle of My Beloved"

Arise, my beloved, my beautiful one and come.
The long winter is past.
The snow has disappeared from the valley.

Rain washed, the green grass glistens.
The poplar, branches lately bared to winter winds,
Clads herself anew in amber green.
Where woodlands hide from human gaze, trillium and violets bloom unseen.
A wand waved over myriad gardens by hand invisible
Commands the color to burst forth.
Plants obey, eager to delight the eye of my beloved…
What then of Him, the Holy Spirit, the Paraclete?
Shall spring be more generous than He?
Can His breath cause less change in the souls of man
Than spring's breath upon the land?
Lift your eyes and look about you.
Souls more numerous than blossoms!
In those souls rare beauty lies enclosed,
To wait the calling forth, the urgency of His command.
His coming is in silence, in the soundlessness that knows no time.
Behold, He makes all things new…
Seeking to find His will in all we do,
Let us run the way to blissful eternity.
Arise! I wait Your coming!
He beckons! Rise, my beloved, and come …

For Prayer and Meditation

1. Make a list of those parts of creation you consider to be most beautiful. Then picturing each one, see if you can hear God telling you that it is a part of him. The same exercise can be done while taking a walk, as a response to everything you see.
2. Ask each creation to reveal to you what its qualities say about the beauty of God.
3. Try to imagine what each natural object might be like in eternity, freed from all defect, our experience of it relieved of all annoying accompaniments such as smog, traffic, dirt. Dwell on these qualities long enough to be able to sense the joy that is awaiting you in the kingdom of heaven.
4. Go on a praise walk from time to time, letting your soul expand with a holy sense of joy in God's gift.
5. Try to find religious pictures which especially appeal to you, perhaps ask family friends to give you such pictures as gifts for Christmas or birthday. You might redecorate your house or room to make it more spiritually

beautiful—perhaps placing your favorite picture in a central position with a candle under it to be lit for prayer and for feast days.

6. What do you imagine your experience of beauty will be in heaven?

7. The poem at the end of this chapter by Sister Dolores was written with the natural beauty of Oregon in mind. Write one of your own using a setting you are familiar with, then take each line as an opening for silent contemplative prayer.

Chapter 4

"Blessed Be The Pure of Heart, For They Shall See God" (Mt. 5:8)

"WHY DON'T YOU GO AWAY for a second honey moon?" an older married couple might be asked. In the case of the very happily wed, the idea is delightful. But for those who have become estranged through the years, no prospect could be more unwelcome. They are living in a sort of detente based on keeping a distance between themselves. Prolonged closer contact would only increase the sense of depression and resentment.

By analogy, Christians whose union with Christ up to the point of death has been close, who have not shrunk from his embrace even in the humiliation of their own sins, but let his sacrificial love heal them, such have seen God's face and long to be with him forever in eternity

To continue the comparison, the impure of heart, we who have fled from God in anger at his strong decrees and at the seemingly harsh turns of his

Providence, who have chosen the immediate gratification of sin and weakness over faith in him, naturally hesitate to come closer to One who is consciously or unconsciously regarded as an adversary.

As with an unhappily married couple, renewal, re-opening, reconciliation, must take place before re-*union* in love can come, so in our relationship to God, we must become pure of heart before we can see his loving Face, in time and in eternity.

> When the Son of Man comes in his glory, escorted by all the angels of heaven, he will sit upon his royal throne, and all the nations will be assembled before him. Then he will separate them into two groups, as a shepherd separates sheep from goats. The sheep he will place on his right hand, the goats on his left.
>
> The king will say to those on his right: "Come. You have my father's blessing! Inherit the kingdom prepared for you from the creation of the world. For I was hungry and you gave me food, I was thirsty and you gave me drink. I was a stranger and you welcomed me, naked and you clothed me. I was ill and you comforted me, in prison and you came to visit

me." Then the just will ask him: "Lord, when did we see you hungry and feed you or see you thirsty and give you drink? When did we welcome you away from home or clothe you in your nakedness? When did we visit you when you were ill or in prison?" The king will answer them: "I assure you, as often as you did it for one of my least brothers, you did it for me."

Then he will say to those on his left: "Out of my sight, you condemned, into that everlasting fire prepared for the devil and his angels! I was hungry and you gave me no food, I was thirsty and you gave me no drink. I was away from home and you gave me no welcome, naked, and you gave me no clothing. I was ill and in prison and you did not come to comfort me." Then they in turn will ask: "Lord, when did we see you hungry or thirsty or away from home or naked, or ill or in prison and not attend you in your needs?" He will answer them: "I assure you, as often as you neglected to do it to one of these least ones, you neglected to do it to me." These will go off to eternal punishment and the just to eternal life. (Mt. 25:31-46)

Such is the purity of heart we are called to in our following of the way of the Lord. I sometimes imagine Jesus as a young man gazing at the beautiful order of nature, then turning back with horror and sadness to the moral chaos of the human scene with its greediness, lust, pride, and indifference. I think of him seeking in prayer for exactly the right words to capture our allegiance to his plan for the new kingdom of love.

Building on the justice of the commandments as the minimum of love, he sought to stretch our hearts with wonderful earthy parables such as the one above about sheep and goats. He wanted to move us to love our neighbors as ourselves, giving generously of our possessions, heaping benefits even on our enemies.

Knowing that times would change, he sent the Holy Spirit of truth to enlighten his Church (Jn. 16:13), in this way to teach how basic Gospel values could be applied to changing circumstances.[6]

---

[6] If the idea of moral authority in the Church is vague to you, it might be good to consult such books as *The*

Further, the Spirit comes directly into our hearts to show us where, by neglect, we have failed to love as deeply and sincerely as the Kingdom requires.

Here is a challenging excerpt from the Exhortations of St. Jane of Chantal to her sisters in the convent, which can be applied to all our relationships:

> We must not be contented to wish them (others) no evil, but we must respect them and wish them all sorts of good and prosperity.... It is not enough to give them no trouble and annoyance, but we must procure their peace of heart, their consolation and joy... Certainly those who read the Holy Scripture see that it is quite full of proofs of the ardent desire which God has that we shall love our neighbor.[7]

Catholic Catechism by John Hardon, Doubleday, 1974, or my own *Christian Ethics in Your Everyday Life*.

[7] *Saint Jane Frances Freymot de Chantal: Her Exhortations, Conferences and Instructions.* Westminster, MD: The Newman Bookshop, 1947, p. 37.

Many images can be given to show how lack of love constricts the heart, making it less open to union with the Sacred Heart. St. John of the Cross taught that a bird tied to a chain cannot fly. But no less can a bird tied with a thin thread. In the same way, whatever is holding us back from holiness keeps us away from the sight of the Savior.

Hence the beginning of purification as a preparation for the vision of God in eternity is confession that so far we have failed to follow his beautiful if difficult way of love.

There is more joy in heaven over one repentant sinner than over ninety-nine righteous people who have no need to repent (Lk. 15:7). Let us then give to those in heaven the joy of seeing us repent, that we might be forgiven and start afresh to try to do the will of God. Let us come to the sacrament of reconciliation gladly.

My own image:

"Act of Contrition"

By night I give you all,
by day 1 take it back,
coin by coin

in miserly egoism.

I hear you call me
hypocrite,
Judas-friend.

No, not true!
For yet I weep
and so You call me
Peter, Magdalene,
dearest daughter,
not evil,
rather weak,
and Mine
no matter what.

May the words be often on our lips: "Jesus, Son of the Living God, have mercy on me a sinner," and "Holy Mary, Mother of God, pray for us sinners now and at the hour of our death."

Contrition must be followed by longing to change our lives that they may become a true following of the way of Christ. In the novel considered by many to be the greatest of all time, *The Brothers Karamazov*, Dostoevsky has a character ask the holy Elder Zossima how to overcome the fear of death, seen as total annihilation.

Surprisingly, the monk offers no philosophical or theological arguments but instead suggests that intellectual doubt can only be remedied by *active love*. As we practice self-donating love even in the face of failure and rejection, we enter into the stream of God's care. Closer to him through this identification with his Heart, we become more aware of the preciousness of the human beings we serve and, indirectly, of our own worth in his eyes. Thomas Aquinas taught succinctly that we can only *love ourselves loving*. In our concern, we activate the part of ourselves which is worthy of our own esteem. Wishing so much for the happiness of those we are trying to help, we come to see how intensely God longs for the day when he can bring all of us into the happiness of heaven. In this way our doubts of immortality fade away.

Becoming pure of heart depends not only on being forgiven but also on forgiving, and not only on forgiving people but also God himself. Like Job of the Old Testament, we sometimes feel overwhelmed by the crosses in our lives. With Jesus in agony we cry out, "My God, my God, why have you forsaken me?" And such anguish comes not only from the "stings and arrows of outrageous fortune" but also from the misery of not being able to save our loved ones from evil, to bring them the happiness we want for them so much.

Only the Father himself can console and reassure us that his love conquers all. Instead of hiding from him in the bitterness of our hearts, we must call upon him from the depths, that he may bring us to a purifying act of total surrender.

Our hearts can also not be pure if we have not forgiven our enemies. Otherwise, the clear stream of love given us in grace is constantly polluted by an evil current of anger.

"Forgive us our trespasses as we forgive those who trespass against us." With those words, we are forced to see that our own eternal salvation depends on completely relinquishing our cherished hates, our delicious feeling of superiority when we pass in review the deeds of our adversaries or the downfall we wish for them. Among the prayer exercises you will find suggestions for praying to be able to forgive.

A poem I once wrote depicts the purification of forgiveness as it opens us to God.

"Cross and Resurrection"

For years I hung on Your cross,
At last so cozy
I made its wood into
The coffin of my dreams!
Now, boldly, You open it,
not afraid of the stench
of old rage.
Tenderly You uncoil the shroud
With Your own hands.
The wounds tear.
Living waters flow
I swim in Your immensity,
Float stunned in Your love.

"Blessed be the pure of heart, for they shall see God." Let us end this chapter with prayers for that purity of heart which will enable us one day to see God.

"Peace Prayer of St. Francis"

Lord, make me an instrument of your peace:
where there is hatred, let me sow love;
where there is injury, pardon;

where there is doubt, faith;
where there is despair, hope;
where there is darkness, light;
where there is sadness, joy.

    O divine Master,
grant that I may not so much seek to be consoled as to console,
to be understood as to understand,
to be loved as to love.
For it is in giving that we receive,
it is in pardoning that we are pardoned,
and it is in dying that we are born to eternal life.

                                                      Amen.

"Prayer of St. Ignatius Loyola"

Take, O Lord, and receive all my liberty, my memory, my understanding, and my whole will. All that I am and all that I possess You have given me. I surrender it all to Your love and Your grace, with these I will be rich enough, and will desire nothing more.

Jesus, Mary and Joseph, I give you my heart and my soul.
Jesus, Mary and Joseph, assist me in my last agony.

Jesus, Mary and Joseph, may I breathe forth my soul in peace with you. Amen.

Chapter 4: "Blessed Be The Pure of Heart…"

For Prayer and Meditation

1. Go through the Scripture and Church teaching making an examination of your own conscience to see where you have failed to follow the way of the Lord.
2. Make a general confession of all the sins of your life in the sacrament of reconciliation or, if this in not available to you, in your own solemn prayer.
3. Try to repeat often the "pray for us sinners, now and at the hour of our death," and "Jesus, Son of the living God, have mercy ort me."
4. Are there any chains or threads that must be cut before you can fly?
5. Meditate on the major sufferings of your life. Open each wound to Christ and offer them in union with the agonies of his heart, accepting the Providence of your Father in heaven.
6. Compose a letter, a dialogue, a poem or a prayer with written or unspoken words, expressing forgiveness for each person in your life whom you feel has hurt you in any way.
7. Pray for total commitment to Christ. Then read the New Testament slowly asking the

Holy Spirit to reveal to you exactly how you might live out the truths of Christ in the present circumstances of your life. You might seek the help of a spiritual director in the course of these reflections.

8. Make it a practice to do spiritual reading each night before going to sleep, giving the Spirit room to inspire you.

Chapter 5

"That Your Joy May Be Full" (Jn.16:24)

"ALL JOY SEEKS ETERNITY" wrote the God-haunted atheist Friedrich Nietzsche. At moments of supreme delight, we say that time stood still: the unforgettable "I love you," the birth of a baby, the rays of the sun shimmering on the sea, the reunion of long separated friends, ecstasy in prayer.

In the *Eighth Symphony* of Gustav Mahler, soaring music accompanies the famous line of Goethe where the redeemed Faust enters heaven to hear the angels singing "all passing things were but an image." Alleluia, we shall shout when we see all our purest earthly joys transfigured in the Kingdom.

Would it not be appropriate in the light of such hope that we spend time in prayer each day letting the thought of eternal joy comfort and uplift us?

Those who picture God exclusively as a cold concept or a frightening judge seem to have passed over too quickly the lines in St. John's Gospel, "I tell You truly: You Will Weep and mourn while the World rejoices; You will grieve for a time, but your grief Will be turned into joy. When a woman is in labor she is sad that her time has come. When she has borne her child, she no longer remembers her pain for joy that a man has been born into the world. In the same way, you are sad for a time, but I shall see you again; then your hearts will rejoice with a joy no one can take from you." (Jn. 16:20-22)

Some joys we foresee and relish beforehand in recurring fantasy. But many come as a surprise. The Apostle Paul tantalizes us with mystical yearning when he proclaims that "Eye has not seen, ear has not heard, nor has it so much as dawned on man what God has prepared for those who love him." (I Cor. 2:9)

One of the greatest surprises I think, will be the sight of our own resurrected transfigured bodies. We repeat in our Creed the words "I believe in the Resurrected Body," yet few seem to find delight in this promise.

I conceive of my resurrected body as light, free, perfectly able to express my spirit, a fulfillment of my image of an earthly dancer's body. It will be a woman's body, in my case, graceful and rounded yet without my own defects. Ageless yet resilient, tangible yet permeable, it will enable me to leap toward whatever attracts me of natural, human, or divine beauty.

In reverie, an analogy came to mind:

"Transfiguration"

Old match
in your dusty box,
who would guess
that struck by human hand
you could yet burst into flame?

Old body
in your fatigues
who would guess
that in the monstrance of God's love
you could shine with glory?

Daydream? Too good to be true? Not according to the Word of God. The Christ who raised Lazarus, who emerged himself from death with a resurrected body, tangible enough to imbibe food and drink, yet capable of walking through doors; who had the body of his mother lifted into heaven; this same Lord promised us in the words of St. Paul:

All of us are to be changed in an instant, in the twinkling of an eye, at the sound of the last trumpet .... This corruptible body must be clothed in incorruptibility... death is swallowed up in victory. O death, where is your sting? (1 Cor. 15:51-55)

As a seed dies in the earth to come forth a full grown plant, "so it is with the resurrection of the dead. What is sown in the earth is subject to decay, what rises is incorruptible. What is sown is ignoble, what rises is glorious .... A natural body is put down and a spiritual body comes up." (I Cor. '15:42-44).

I happened to be reading a lot of Caryll Houselander at the time of writing this book, and so I am quoting her frequently. Here are some lines from a poem entitled "The Spirit Speaks to the Body on the Day of Resurrection":

Come back to me,
you beloved,
who have gathered the beauty of the earth
to the unchanging
through centuries of change.

Chapter 5: "That Your Joy May Be Full"

God has put off the universe
like a cloak worn threadbare,
and made new his raiment ...
Body I love,
fallen away into grey dust,
heart of my little love,
a handful of dust
grown in the blossom
of flowers upon the grave,
down in windblown seed
all over the earth…

Strength of beauty
is there now in the filigree
of your bleached bones,
little skeleton
that were the pillars
of Christ's lowliest house—
will they bring me the living wood
of the almond tree...
and your tongue,
will it sing with all the
winds and the wild birds' song?

When you died
they folded your hands on the crucifix
over your heart,
and composed your blameless feet
and buried you under the earth.

Come,
God's glory
burning in me
will burn in you
and you will shine in His light
as the moon in the light of the sun:

Come,
I will live in you
as the bridegroom lives
in the life of the bride.[8]

Many will be the joys of heaven. A lover of novels, I once came to realize that writers of fiction exercise a redemptive function. No matter how terrible a hero

---

[8] From *Caryll Houselander: That Divine Eccentric*, by Maisie Ward, NY: Sheed and Ward, 1962, pp. 326-329.

or heroine, by showing us all the suffering or emptiness which led up to the horrendous deed, the author causes us to feel compassion, And so I imagine that part of our heaven will be to trace the ins and outs of God's grace in the lives of every person he redeemed, that we may rejoice in the miracles of salvation.

The concept of eternity as a resting place, a final home, is one which imparts sweet longing for heaven. On the way to a strange place, I thought once of the words of Christ, "In my house there are many mansions .... I go to prepare a place for you." (Jn. 14:2-3) What a cozy image! Would I be afraid to visit a house where my husband had gone before, decorating it exactly to my taste, as guests inviting my favorite people?

Still more intimately, what joy comes to my heart at the thought of being free to love all those most dear to me including all the saints, without restraint, free from the sins and faults which now cause turmoil or separation.

St. Thomas Aquinas believed that our greatest joy in heaven would be simply the vision of God. Occasionally in contemplation, I can see with an interior eye something of the glory of God. More intense even than the beauty of color or form, this is but the vaguest glimpse of the fullness of his being. Yet the Word in whom we live and move and have our being (Acts 17:28) has promised us that one day we shall see the Father and be perfectly united with him. (Jn. 17:3).

Much easier it is to picture heaven as the embrace of the Christ we have adored in visual form so many years symbolically on the crucifixes of our churches. Oh, when shall that great day come when I, like Mary Magdalene, will rush to kiss the feet of him who died that my joy might be full?

Chapter 5: "That Your Joy May Be Full"

For Prayer and Meditation

1. Consider your moments of greatest joy. Savor them. Try to imagine God's joy in giving you these gifts. Now meditate on the way each of these joys will be fulfilled in heaven.
2. Write a dialogue, prayer, story, or draw a picture, depicting your resurrected body.
3. Meditate on or write about the way God has brought goodness along the winding paths of your life so far.
4. Picture yourself in your heavenly home embracing all those you have loved on earth. Compose a prayer of thanksgiving for the unique goodness of each of these relatives or friends and for the happiness you anticipate in your perfect union with them in eternity.
5. What does the phrase "I shall see the face of God" mean to you? In silent contemplation let God lead you more deeply into the glory of his being.

Chapter 6

"Perfect Love Casts Out Fear" (1 Jn. 4:18)

A DEAR, VERY DEVOUT FRIEND thought he was nearing his time of death. Trying to get close to what he might be feeling, I wrote a series of short prayer-poems. As you read them, you might think about which lines correspond to your own thoughts.

"Old Pilgrim"

Why tarriest thou
atop the last mountain?
What mysteries yet to be fulfilled?

Joyfully
to hear the voices of children
singing your songs in the valley?

Sorrowfully
to feel every bone crushed
under the weight of the world?

Gloriously
to wait 'til the mists clear
for Elijah's chariot
to carry you to Abraham's bosom?

"The wind blows
The sea flows
And God only knows."[9]

"Tunnel of Love"

Digging through
The tunnel of time,
Sometimes I hear
Your song loudly,
sometimes faint.
Sometimes my own
is weak,
sometimes a
Full-throated cry.

When we meet

---

[9] From *Portrait of Jennie*, by Robert Nathan.

Chapter 6: "Perfect Love Casts Out Fear"

no more signals.
Deep silence
as You carry me
to eternity!

"Together Forever"

In the end,
I shall have no foothold,
only hand-hold.
Teach me, Lord,
how to hold hands
in the dark.

"Whither?"

Floating out to sea
on a raft of Your love.
What is Your will, my Lord,
that I come further,
further out,
or that I swim
against the tide
back to shore?

Now I lay me down
to sleep
in the grave of time
and cry
Eternity!

> "Ascension"

first the head dreams eternity
then the heart beats eternity
then the will clasps eternity
last the limbs leap eternity

The last poem of the series ended with the Scripture on which this chapter is based:

> "Day and Night"

By day You breathe me out.
By night You breath me back
into Your heart.
When will this rhythm end?
And when it does

will I be out of in?
"Perfect Love Casts Out Fear"

> As the Father has loved me, so I have loved you. Live on in my love... All this I tell you that my joy may be yours and your joy may be complete... It was not you who chose me, it was I who chose you... love one another. (Jn. 15:9-17)

> Anyone who loves me will be true to my word, and my Father will love him; we will come to him and make our dwelling place with him. (Jn. 14:23)

How can we believe that God is love yet fear we will be cast off, never to be drawn into full unity with him? It is the very essence of love to seek unity:

> My sheep hear my voice. I know them, and they follow me. I give them eternal life, and they shall never perish. No one shall snatch them out of my hand. My Father is greater than all, in what he has given me, and there is

no snatching out of his hand. The Father and I are one. (Jn. 10:27-30)

And, even more graphically:

I do not pray for them alone. I pray also for those who will believe in me through their word, that all may be one as you, Father, are in me, and I in you; I pray that they may be [one] in us, that the world may believe that you sent me. I have given them the glory you gave me that they may be one, as we are one—I living in them, you living in me—that their unity may be complete. So shall the world know that you sent me, and that you loved them as you loved me. Father, all those you gave me I would have in my company where I am, to see this glory of mine which is your gift to me, because of the love you bore me before the world began. Just Father, the world has not known you, but I have known you; and these men have known that you sent me. To them I have revealed your name, and I will continue to reveal it so that your love for me

Chapter 6: "Perfect Love Casts Out Fear"

may live in them, and I may live in them. (Jn. 17:20-26)

We read these words. We are deeply comforted. Yet a slight fear still remains. If God loves us so much, why did he make the door to his home so dark? Why reduce us to such helplessness? Why torture us with such pain in the body and anguish in the mind as a prelude to our deliverance?

Words alone cannot answer these questions but only in surrender to Christ, identifying with his cry, "My God, my God, why have you forsaken me?" (Mt. 27:46), entrusting his loved ones to each other (Jn. 19:26-27), "I thirst" (Jn. 19:28), and finally repeating with him, "Father, into your hands I commend my spirit." (Lk. 23:46)

The word "commend" means to place something in safekeeping, so when we die we place our souls into the hands of God for safekeeping.

In any serious illness, because we are weakened and subject to despair, and also because we might be at death's door, it is recommended that we call on the priest for the sacrament of anointing. This will bring us healing graces and also strengthen us spiritually. If we were more confident of life after death, we would not be afraid to ask for the sacrament of anointing for ourselves and others dear to us. How beautiful are the words of anointing: "Let us pray to the Lord for our sick brother (sister) and for all those dedicated to serving and caring for him (her). Look kindly on our sick brother (sister)… Give new strength to his (her) body and mind… Ease our brother's (sister's) sufferings …. Free him (her) from sin and temptation…"

When very near to death, the priest brings Holy Communion and says the words, "Lord, you are the source of eternal health for those who believe in you. May our brother (sister) N., who has been refreshed with food and drink from heaven, safely reach your kingdom of light and life."

Many Catholics like to recite the prayers of the Rosary over and over again as they are dying. The holy Pope Pius XII, however, also asked to hear his favorite music. I, too, find that the glorious music of the great composers gives me a glimpse of victory over death. Listening to Bach's *B Minor Mass*, Beethoven's *Missa Solemnis*, Verdi's *Requiem* seems to open the heavens. Such music reminds me of the words of St. Teresa of Avila, who at one time when she was young seemed to have died, and while being prepared for burial, arose on her bier. She told her friends that "death is ecstasy."

"Only he who becomes as a little child will enter the kingdom of heaven" (Mt. 18:2-3). Perhaps this is why God often brings us to him after reducing us to a childlike state of helplessness:

> It seems that most people return to their childhood in those last hours. It is one more manifestation of Eternal Pity, that even the seeming lost, the worldly wise, the unregenerate, often do in the end become as little children, to suffer the last agony with the wholeness of a child's capacity, and so be able, after all, to enter the kingdom of heaven.[10]

Death, first experienced as a stranger, then an enemy, finally is greeted as friend, lover, and mother as Peter Kreeft wrote in his wonderful book *Love is*

---

[10] Caryll Houselander, *The Dry Wood*, p. 222.

Stronger than Death.[11] Hence the prayers of the dying are gentle and childlike:

> Hail Mary, full of grace, the Lord is with you. Blessed are you among women, and blessed is the fruit of your womb, Jesus. Holy Mary, Mother of God, pray for us sinners now and at the hour of our death. Amen.

> Soul of Christ, sanctify me;
> Body of Christ, save me;
> Blood of Christ, inebriate me;
> Water from the side of Christ, wash me;
> Passion of Christ, strengthen me.
> O good Jesus, hear me;
> Within your wounds hide me;
> Separated from you, let me never be;
> From the evil one protect me;
> At the hour of my death, call me;
> And close to you bid me;
> That with your saints I may be,
> Praising you forever and ever. Amen

---

[11] NY: Harper and Row.

I am writing this book at the Franciscan Retreat House of Our Lady of Peace in Oregon, and I would like, therefore, to end it with a passage from the great Franciscan, St. Bonaventure:

Mystical wisdom is revealed by the Holy Spirit

> Christ is both the way and the door. Christ is the staircase and the vehicle, like the *throne of mercy over the Ark of the Covenant*, and *the mystery hidden from the ages*. A man should turn his full attention to this throne of mercy, and should gaze at him hanging on the cross, full of faith, hope and charity, devoted, full of wonder and joy, marked by gratitude, and open to praise and jubilation. Then such a man will make with Christ a *pasch*, that is, a passing-over. Through the branches of the cross he will pass over the Red Sea, leaving Egypt and entering the desert. There he will taste the hidden manna, and rest with Christ in the sepulcher, as if he were dead to things outside. He will experience, as much as is possible for one who is still living, what was

promised to the thief who hung beside Christ: *Today you will be with me in paradise.*

For this passover to be perfect, we must suspend all the operations of the mind and we must transform the peak of our affections, directing them to God alone. This is a sacred mystical experience. It cannot be comprehended by anyone unless he surrenders himself to it; nor can he surrender himself to it unless he longs for it; nor can he long for it unless the Holy Spirit, whom Christ sent into the world, should come and inflame his innermost soul. Hence the Apostle says that this mystical wisdom is revealed by the Holy Spirit.

If you ask how such things can occur, seek the answer in God's grace, not in doctrine; in the longing of will, not in the understanding; in the sighs of prayer, not in research; seek the bridegroom not the teacher; God and not man; darkness not daylight; and look not to the light but rather to the raging fire that carries the soul to God with intense fervor and glowing love. The fire is God, and the furnace is in Jerusalem, fired by Christ in the ardor of his loving passion. Only he understood this who said: *My soul chose hanging and my bones death.* Anyone who cherishes this kind of death can see God, for it is certainly true that: *No man can look upon me and live.*

Let us die, then, and enter into the darkness, silencing our anxieties, our passions and all the fantasies of our imagination. Let us pass over with the crucified Christ *from this world to the Father*, so that when the Father has shown himself to us, we can say with Philip: *It is enough.* We may hear with Paul: *My grace is sufficient for you*; and we can rejoice with David, saying: *My flesh and my heart fail me, but God is the strength of my heart and my heritage for ever. Blessed be the Lord for ever, and let all the people say: Amen. Amen!*

For Prayer and Meditation

1. Take out lines from the poems in this chapter to lead you into prayer, or form your own images to write down or to draw.
2. Read the Scriptures included in this chapter very slowly inserting your own name so that you
3. can begin to hear the Father expressing his love for you with the voice of his Son.
4. Read the Scriptures about the last days of Jesus, or make the Stations of the Cross identifying yourself in your fears about death with the sufferings and ultimate abandonment of Christ: (Mt. 27; Mk.13-15; Lk. 22:39, all of 23; Jn. 18-19).
5. Now read the accounts of the Resurrection imagining that it is your own rising, with you being welcomed in heaven.
6. Listen, play, or sing music about the Resurrection. You may try soft celestial Gregorian Chant, melodious classical works, or comforting popular hymns such as *Swing Low, Sweet Chariot*.

7. Read the prayers given at the end of the chapter selecting those you would like to recite often, or making up your own.
8. Add passages you find about heaven to the end of your booklet of responses, or make some into bookmarks for yourself and your friends.

†††

May all who read this book pray for its author that we may all meet in heaven one day to rejoice in our victory over death in the arms of Our Savior.

www.ingramcontent.com/pod-product-compliance
Lightning Source LLC
Chambersburg PA
CBHW060852050426
42453CB00008B/945